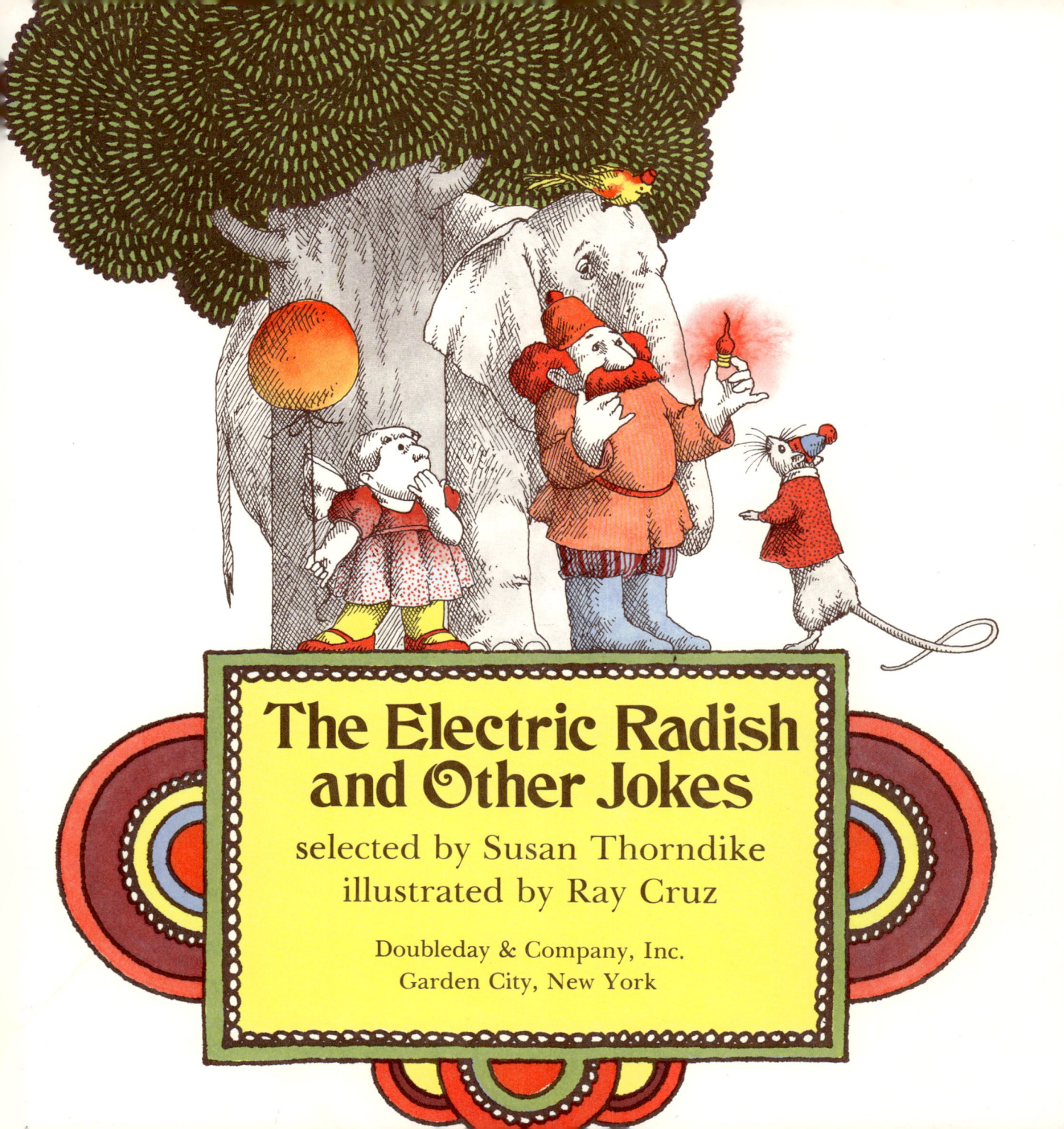

The Electric Radish and Other Jokes

selected by Susan Thorndike
illustrated by Ray Cruz

Doubleday & Company, Inc.
Garden City, New York

Library of Congress Catalog Card Number 75-183615
Illustrations © 1973 by Ray Cruz
All Rights Reserved
Printed in the United States of America
First Edition

What is red, has a tail, and hums?

An electric radish.

Here, kitty, kitty, kitty.

Who invented gunpowder?

A woman who wanted cannons to look pretty.

Mother Kangaroo: Oh no! I've had my pocket picked!

Boy: None, but I want to grow some.

Mother tiger to baby tiger: What are you doing?
Baby tiger: I'm chasing a hunter around a tree.

Mother tiger: How often do I have to tell you not to play with your food?

What goes 999 thump, 999 thump, 999 thump?

A centipede with a wooden leg.

A lost camel.

Because they have two left feet.

He sits on a leaf
and waits for the fall.

How does a monster count to 17?

On his fingers.

Why did the elephant paint his toenails red?

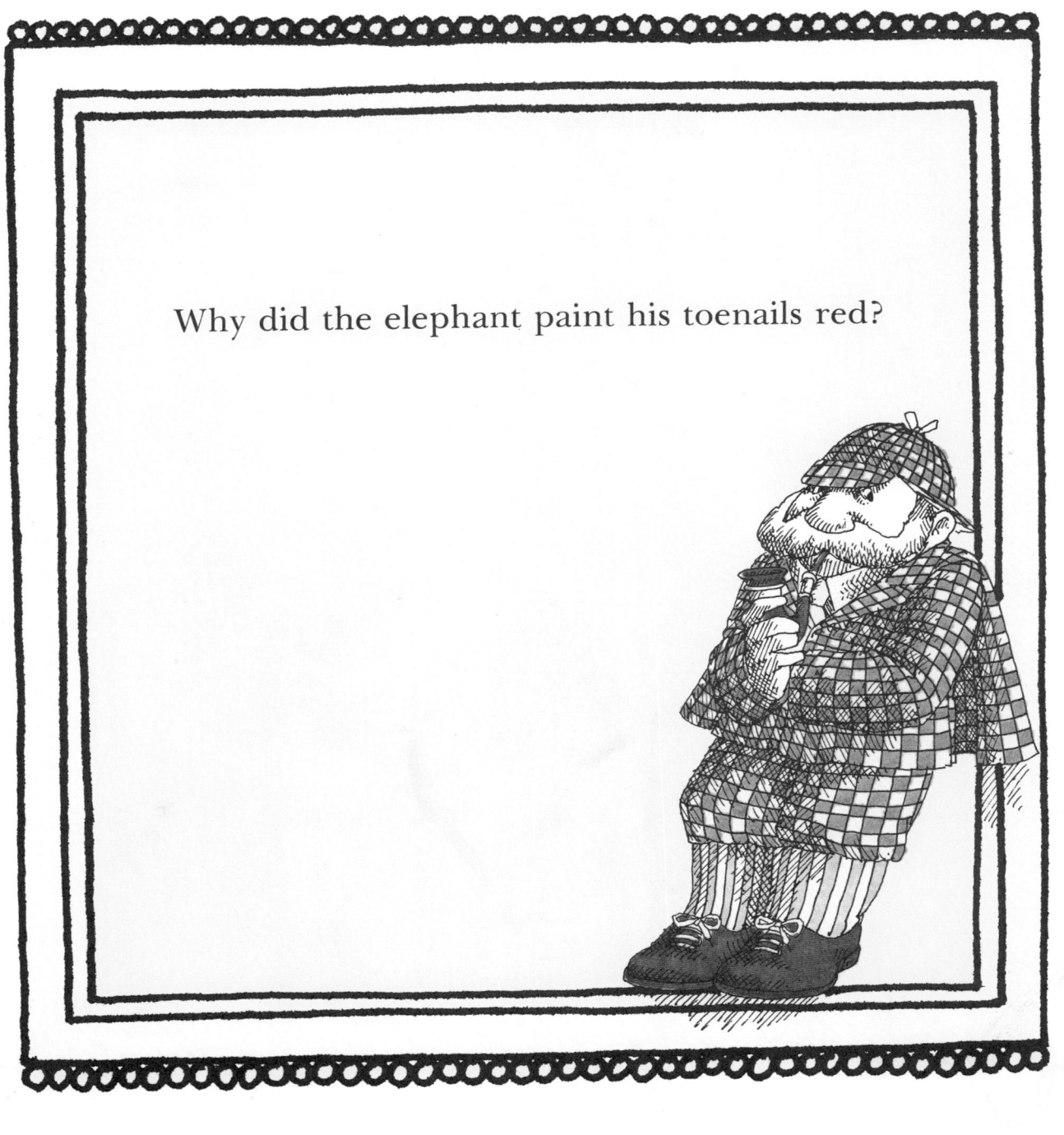

What is the best way to catch a squirrel?

Sit in a tree and act like a nut.

Why is a rabbit's nose always shiny?

Because his powder puff is on the wrong end.

How does a hippopotamus get up a tree?

Climbs on an acorn and waits.

What do you do with a blue monster?

Cheer him up.

Teacher: Frankie, can you define nonsense?

Frankie: An elephant hanging over a cliff with his tail tied to a buttercup

If April showers bring May flowers,
what do May flowers bring?

Pilgrims.

Why does the elephant wear dark glasses?

If you had all those jokes told about you, you wouldn't want to be recognized either.

What is yellow and green and eats grass?
    A yellow and green grass-eater.

What is yellow and blue and eats grass?
    A yellow and blue grass-eater?

Nope, they only come in yellow and green.

Susan Thorndike received her B.A. in English and American literature from Brandeis University and prepared THE ELECTRIC RADISH AND OTHER JOKES while working at Doubleday & Company in the children's book department. She lives in New York City and in her spare time is learning to make pottery.

Ray Cruz, a native New Yorker, attended the High School of Art and Design, Pratt Institute, and Cooper Union and has been drawing all his life. He has illustrated a number of books, including THE STORYBOOK COOKBOOK, HORRIBLE HEPZIBAH, MARVELOUS MACHINES, and GREAT QUILLOW. Mr Cruz lives in Greenwich Village.

MINNEAPOLIS PUBLIC LIBRARY

Please leave the transaction and book cards in this pocket.

The borrower is responsible for all materials drawn on his card and for fines on overdue items. Marking and mutilation of books are prohibited, and are punishable by law.

WASHBURN
1973